I0357085

Tapestry of Creation
Oracle Flipbook

Rachel White

How to use this book...

Each page contains guidance for you to contemplate and muse with until you arrive at your own inner wisdom. Trust your intuitive interpretation for each piece of guidance. You are the oracle and this book is simply a tool for you to tune into your own inner guidance.

To receive guidance, hold the book to your heart and tune into what question you have or area you would like insight into - flip to the page you feel called to stop on and read the words you land on.

You may play with this book however you like, allow your creative impulse to lead the way.

The blank space around the words is for you to add colour and imagery however you would like to.

Have have as you play inside.

Love,
Rachel

xx

The guidance within this book is derived from the topics and themes explored within the book Tapestry of Creation, if you would love a more in depth exploration of what you read within this oracle flipbook, get yourself a copy.

*Trust in your capacity to create. Your life-force energy **is** your creative energy*

Adopt a beginner's mind - how can you look at this situation with fresh eyes and no preconceived beliefs or ideas?

~ 3 ~

Follow your own impulses - go inwards to find that magical guidance you are seeking

~ 4 ~

This is the permission slip
you have been hoping for

~ 5 ~

Make space for reverence and devotion when it comes to your art

Play with imitating the art of others to discover the mediums of art that you enjoy

*Play with innovation - how
can you add artistic value
to something existing?*

*Something fresh and original wants
to emerge through you - give yourself
the space to play and rest in order
for this vision to clearly manifest*

*You are the only one who can
see through your eyes and
imagination - make your
moves based on what you see.
Allow the opinions of others to
dissolve when it comes to your
creative vision*

Are you listening to the whispers? An idea wants to come to life through you, are you willing to hear it?

~ 11 ~

Align with life to align with your next creative idea - stop trying and get back to living

Honour the double mission -
creating for your joy AND
creating for service to all

The journey is the fulfilling part
- widen your view to see more
than the narrow end result

*Mistakes and bumps in the road
are part of the journey - offer
yourself grace and forgiveness and
then allow yourself to move forward*

You are safe to create

Complete the creative cycle
- it is important that you
see this all the way through

*Look at where you are
holding on to this feeling
hard - it is meant to feel easy*

Re-examine your beliefs about your creativity and where they came from - it is time to reprogram your mind to hold more empowering beliefs about your creative potential

~ 19 ~

Yes - you know what to do

~ 20 ~

No - you know you don't want this

*The world is your muse - go outside
and see inspiration is everywhere*

*Widen your view to
see the big picture*

Put on your rose coloured glasses and allow space for the romanticisation of life

This situation needs further contemplation - when you give soft space to ponder on the situation, the solution or further insight will naturally emerge

Transcend the
intimidation you are
feeling into inspiration

~ 26 ~

Pour magic into the mundane - let something that often feels boring to be artful today!

*Use your own hands to
make something beautiful*

Contrast is needed right now - do something new and different today to give contrast to your daily life

New ideas will meet you when you are moving - stay in motion to build momentum in your creative pursuits

To filter through the many creative ideas you have, remind yourself of your highest values and priorities

~ 31 ~

Connect with what feels fun

You are incredibly resourceful, you have all you need within to gather all you need to bring your creation to life

~ 33 ~

*This idea may be for
someone else, trust your
impulse to offer ideas back
out into the world*

~ 34 ~

This *is your sign*

Gaze within what you see,
what hidden art will your
artistry reveal to the world?

Wouldn't it be great if...

(use this prompt to entice new thoughts and ideas out)

*Take some time to honour the
sacred roots of your creations
and life. Where can you trace
back the lineage?*

~ 38 ~

*Delight in this moment by
letting go of the seriousness -
make more space for lightness,
humour, and play*

~ 39 ~

Play

~ 40 ~

Rest

~ 41 ~

All in divine timing

Bring yourself back into your natural rhythm by connecting with nature

Your creative expression is
time expanding - stop using
time as an excuse and allow
it to be on your side

*Stop interfering - plant the
seeds and trust they will
grow without you digging
them up to check*

*Distractions will fade away
when you follow the art that
makes you feel alive*

*Embracing your creative nature
will open your channel for inspired
insight and divine wisdom*

*Meditate on this concern -
bring yourself into an alpha
(relaxed) state and the way
forward will become clear*

Your creations are valuable and worth creating even when others do not recognise the brilliance

*Your legacy spans far beyond
this moment, don't get caught
up in the criticism or praise of
what you just created*

*Allow what you have
done to be enough*

*Cultivate a practice
of sacred laziness*

Boundaries are needed here

*Your boundaries are restricting
you and syphoning your energy -
re-evaluate what boundaries are
needed and how much energy
you need to give them*

*You get to choose how you think
and feel within this moment of
your story - even when the
situation is beyond your control
remember that you influence how
you experience this moment*

*This disruption to your
creative rhythm is serving
to the bigger picture*

*Your action will be met
with effortless flow -
take the first step*

~ 57 ~

There is no rush, you have
all the time that you need

*Extend your breath to
extend your life-force and
creativity - pause to take
some deep breaths*

*All is well - invite in
softness around the stress
and resistance*

Your evolution is part of the collective evolution - you bringing your creations to life and journeying through that part of your story is serving to all

*Tune into the codes in your body
that are ready to be activated,
your body knows the way*

~ 62 ~

Look for the sacred truth within
the symbolism and stories

~ 63 ~

Reconnect to your stability
through your breath, slow
down and breathe

*Your boundaries are not
meant to be electric fences,
contemplate your boundaries
that may be restricting you*

~ 65 ~

What distance do you need to
love yourself and the other?

*Embrace your flowing and
playful nature, let yourself
create with no structure or rules*

There is a need for more structure, give your creativity a stronger landing place

~ 68 ~

*Embrace the archetype of your
inner young maiden - how
would she see and move
through this situation with her
enthusiasm and ambition?*

Embrace the archetype of your inner mother - how would she see and move through this situation through her nurturing and protective lens?

Embrace the archetype of your inner enchantress - how would she see and move through this situation with her potent power?

Embrace the archetype of your inner crone - how would she see and move through this situation with her mature wisdom?

*Honour the season you are
in and know that this
season shall pass, how can
you honour where you are?*

*There is light in the void
you have found yourself in
- are you willing to see it?*

Honour your relationship with your sexuality for it is reflective of your relationship with you creativity

~ 75 ~

Allow yourself to receive by
embracing that prosperity
is your birth-right

*Listen to what your
emotions are revealing to
you - trust the messages
and act accordingly*

Your body's sensations are guiding you - listen to the pulse of your clit, butterflies in your stomach, and all other visceral feelings

Before rebirth there must be death, what are you clinging to that needs to die?

*Trace back through your
lineage for answers, there
are many answers in the
stories of the past*

*Flirt with life and
life will flirt back*

Stop trying to penetrate before the foreplay, to make a creative baby with the universe allow the entire journey to be enjoyable without skipping any steps

You co-created with the universe,
trust that your creations are
supported by a divine force

The soul of your creations
chose you to bring them to
life - trust in your decision
making. Make a decision
and keep moving

This is the labour of love -
remind yourself why you
are here as you face your
final obstacles

*You are both strong and
soft - embrace the polarity
of your experience*

*You have a direct link to
Source, allow yourself to be
an open channel*

*Embrace your divine
essence, you are supported*

Play with this idea within your
third eye and imagination

*Speak your truth, your voice
has a powerful resonance*

Fall in love with your own voice by listening to it with more loving ears

Your heart is calling you into deeper acceptance of what is - can you offer yourself tenderness in this time?

*Your inner child wants to
be involved in this process -
allow her out to play*

You are capable and competent
as you are - fuel your confidence
with this knowing

Give yourself the encouragement you yearned for as a child

~ 95 ~

You made the right decision.
Keep moving forward

Momentum is
catching up with you

*Enjoy the sweetness of being
alive, all else can wait*

~ 98 ~

*Ground yourself by spending
more time in nature*

Accept that there will be times
you will be misunderstood by
others, you are a polarising force.
For some to deeply understand
you others must misunderstand
you, and vice versa

Pay closer attention to how divine totality is reflected in you and your life, to feel closer to your divinity go and look in a mirror

Look to the challenges that are
continually arising through
your life and face what you
have been resisting, you are
safe to face your shadows

Allow yourself to enjoy what
you enjoy, and take pleasure
in your enjoyment of just that

Your shadows only seem like monsters when you are hiding them in the dark, allow these parts of you into the light to see the gift within them

*Use your fear as a portal
into excitement*

Use your shame as a portal into deeper empathy and authentic artistry

Use your anger as a portal
into passion

*Use your frustration as a
portal into a wider
perspective*

*Use your jealousy as a
portal into inspiration and
resourcefulness*

Your pain is sacred fuel for
your art, feel the pain and
harness it into your
creative expression

Let them be uncomfortable in the face of your art, it is serving to them even when they don't feel that way yet

The full embodiment of your depth can only be experienced through your body, spend some time connecting to your physicality

Start with what you do know, begin at the surface thread and pull on it to unravel the mystery underneath

*Life is provoking you to set
more of you free, consider
what life may be trying to
wake you up to*

Play with your visionary imagination, if there were absolutely no limits what would you be doing differently? Take inspiration from your imagination for what you are able to implement today

Stop allowing your past art to limit your next work of art

*Allow yourself to evolve
through the creation of your
art and the living of your life,
your art has value even when
you evolve past it*

*Evaluate where your dreams
have come from - there is
perhaps a dream that came
from someone else that it is
time for you to let go of*

*Whatever you think you should
do is only something you should
do if you want to do it*

Own your story by telling it yourself, using whatever medium of art you feel most fitting

Consider your words wisely - there is just as much power in what you intentionally choose to not say, as the power in what you do say

Your inner child is craving
more wild unpredictable
spontaneity

All of your multidimensional nature wants to shine, let the light through

Creation is a spiritual practice. The creation of your art is a divine act, treat it as such

*No relationship with the
divine is superior to another,
embrace the way you relate to
your own divinity*

Your liberation is serving to the liberation of all. Embrace your place in the collective story

You are one in billions and billions. There is literally no one else that has been created like you. The same creative energy that made you runs through your veins. The art you bring into the world is art that only you can create

When you allow yourself to be different, you allow yourself to connect with the unity of all

Your art is your footprint through the energetic fabric of the world, each step is a part of your legacy. Take a moment to recognise the vastness and the impact of your art has across time and space

Add colour to your life with a little spice and drama, see the sacredness in the drama

Spend today fully embodying
'main character' energy

~ 131 ~

*See the conflict you are
experiencing as an opportunity for
character development, how can
you grow through the conflict?*

*Infuse all moments of
today with your devotional
art, there is no pressure to
attain or achieve anything*

*Create something
beautiful to look at today*

*Embrace a poetic lens in
the way you view your life
and life itself today*

The greatest story ever told is the one you are fully living - look at the ways you can feel more alive today

*May you feel just how
creative you are, in your
blood, bones, and heart*

May you trust in your creative
impulses, letting them guide
you to make a start

*May you always sense the
synchronicities and the
abundance of time and space*

*May you express yourself
freely, liberate your voice,
create at your own sacred pace*

~ 140 ~

*May you know that you are
worthy, that you are creative
beyond any measure*

May you be willing to
explore the full depth of life,
the pain, and all the pleasure

May you embrace that you are Source manifested, that creation is part of you

~ 143 ~

May you see that the beauty
of your art is everywhere, in
all you say and do

*May you know you are
innately creative, this is
definitively true*

*May your creative story of
evolution be one that you
keep moving through*

May you live your life and
create your masterpiece like
everything is a work of art

~ 147 ~

*May you know you are within
the cosmic web of creation; you
are a divine part*

www.ingramcontent.com/pod-product-compliance
Lightning Source LLC
Chambersburg PA
CBHW040240010526
44107CB00065B/2810